MONTANA

The Treasure State

BY
JOHN HAMILTON

Abdo & Daughters

An imprint of Abdo Publishing | abdopublishing.com

abdopublishing.com

Published by ABDO Publishing, a division of ABDO, PO Box 398166, Minneapolis, Minnesota 55439. Copyright © 2017 by Abdo Consulting Group, Inc. International copyrights reserved in all countries. No part of this book may be reproduced in any form without written permission from the publisher. ABDO & Daughters™ is a trademark and logo of ABDO Publishing.

Printed in the United States of America, North Mankato, Minnesota.
032016
092016

Editor: Sue Hamilton   **Contributing Editor:** Bridget O'Brien
Graphic Design: Sue Hamilton
Cover Art Direction: Candice Keimig   **Cover Photo Selection:** Neil Klinepier
Cover Photo: iStock
Interior Images: Airphoto, Alamy, AP, Billings Mustangs, City of Troy, Corbis, C.W. Peale/Independence National Historical Park, David Olson, Dreamstime, Edward S. Paxson/Montana Historical Society, Getty, Glow Images, Granger Collection, Great Falls Voyagers, Helena Brewers, History in Full Color-Restoration/Colorization, iStock, Jerry Ting, John F. Clymer/Clymer Museum of Art, John Hamilton, Johnathon Esper, Karl Bodmer, Katie LaSalle-Lowery, Library of Congress, Mile High Maps, Missoula Osprey, Montana Dept. of Transportation, Montana Office of Tourism, New York Public Library, One Mile Up, Richard Lorenz, Roger Peterson, and University of Montana-Bozeman.

Statistics: *State and City Populations*, U.S. Census Bureau, July 1, 2015/2014 estimates; *Land and Water Area*, U.S. Census Bureau, 2010 Census, MAF/TIGER database; *State Temperature Extremes*, NOAA National Climatic Data Center; *Climatology and Average Annual Precipitation*, NOAA National Climatic Data Center, 1980-2015 statewide averages; *State Highest and Lowest Points*, NOAA National Geodetic Survey.

Websites: To learn more about the United States, visit booklinks.abdopublishing.com. These links are routinely monitored and updated to provide the most current information available.

Cataloging-in-Publication Data

Names: Hamilton, John, 1959- author.
Title: Montana / by John Hamilton.
Description: Minneapolis, MN : Abdo Publishing, [2017] | Series: The United
    States of America | Includes index.
Identifiers: LCCN 2015957613 | ISBN 9781680783285 (lib. bdg.) |
    ISBN 9781680774320 (ebook)
Subjects: LCSH: Montana--Juvenile literature.
Classification: DDC 978.6--dc23
LC record available at http://lccn.loc.gov/2015957613

CONTENTS

THE
TREASURE
STATE

Montana is nicknamed "The Treasure State" because of its mother lode of gold, silver, and other precious minerals buried under the Earth's crust. Montana's other nickname is "Big Sky Country." The state's craggy mountains, forests, and wide-open plains make the horizon seem to disappear into an endless field of blue. Sometimes, when standing on a mountain peak or driving down a lonely prairie road, it seems as if you have the whole state to yourself.

Montana has a colorful history. It is home to many Native American tribes. The Lewis and Clark Expedition traveled through the area in the early 1800s. Sprawling cattle ranches, gold rushes, and copper mines gave Montana a Western flavor, despite its location in the northern United States.

Today, many visitors travel to Montana. Glacier National Park, grizzly bears, soaring mountains, and prairie sunsets are just a few examples of the state's spectacular natural beauty.

Montana's wide-open spaces have led to its nickname: "Big Sky Country."

QUICK FACTS

MONTANA

Name: Montana is taken from the Spanish word *montaña,* meaning "mountain," or "mountainous country."

State Capital: Helena, population 29,943

Date of Statehood: November 8, 1889 (41st state)

Population: 1,032,949 (44th-most populous state)

Area (Total Land and Water): 147,040 square miles (380,832 sq km), 4th-largest state

Largest City: Billings, population 108,869

Nicknames: The Treasure State; Big Sky Country

Motto: *Oro y plata* (Gold and Silver)

State Bird: Western Meadowlark

 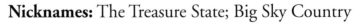

State Flower: Bitterroot

State Gemstone: Sapphire and Agate

State Tree: Ponderosa Pine

Sapphire & Agate

State Song: "Montana"

Highest Point: Granite Peak, 12,799 feet (3,901 m)

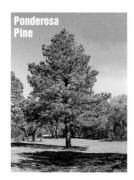

Ponderosa Pine

Lowest Point: Kootenai River, 1,800 feet (549 m)

Average July High Temperature: 81°F (27°C)

Record High Temperature: 117°F (47°C), in Medicine Lake on July 5, 1937

Granite Peak

Average January Low Temperature: 11°F (-12°C)

Record Low Temperature: -70°F (-57°C), at Rogers Pass on January 20, 1954

Kootenai River

Average Annual Precipitation: 19 inches (48 cm)

Number of U.S. Senators: 2

Greetings from MONTANA

usa37

Number of U.S. Representatives: 1

U.S. Postal Service Abbreviation: MT

QUICK FACTS

GEOGRAPHY

Covering 147,040 square miles (380,832 sq km), Montana is the fourth-largest state in the United States. It shares its northern border with Canada. To the east are North Dakota and South Dakota. Wyoming is to the south, while Idaho is to the west.

The source of the Missouri River is in western Montana. It flows eastward across the state until crossing into North Dakota. From there, the river continues southeast until eventually emptying into the Mississippi River in the state of Missouri. Other major rivers in Montana include the Clark Fork and Yellowstone Rivers.

The beginning of the Missouri River is in Montana.

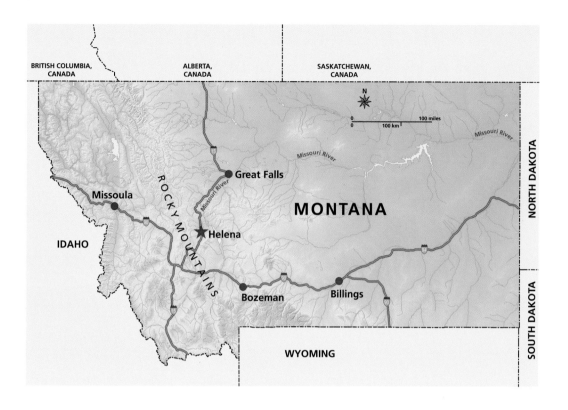

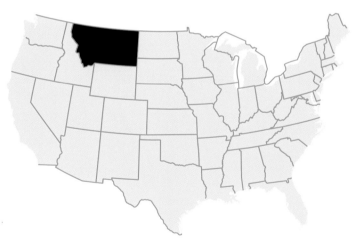

Montana's total land and water area is 147,040 square miles (380,832 sq km). It is the 4th-largest state. The state capital is Helena.

Montana has two main regions, the mountainous west and the plains of the east. The plains occupy about three-fifths of the state. In this area are flat plains and gently rolling hills. It is part of the larger Great Plains region of the west-central United States. The arid land is mostly filled with wheat fields and prairie grasses, although it is interrupted in some places by eroded badlands or isolated low mountains.

Montana's western mountain region occupies about two-fifths of the state. It is filled with thousands of jagged peaks, clustered in dozens of mountain ranges.

Saint Mary Lake
in Glacier National Park.

Together, they are all part of the Rocky Mountains of North America, which stretch from Canada all the way south to New Mexico. The word *montaña* in the Spanish language means "mountain," or "mountainous country."

Montana's tallest point is Granite Peak, which towers 12,799 feet (3,901 m) high. It is in the Beartooth Mountains of south-central Montana. Nearby is Yellowstone National Park, part of which lies in the state (although the majority of the park is in Wyoming).

In Montana's northwestern corner is Glacier National Park. It contains more than one million acres (404,686 ha) of wilderness, 650 lakes, glaciers, and alpine meadows. The Continental Divide runs down the middle of the park, then travels south through Montana before exiting the state.

CLIMATE AND WEATHER

Because of Montana's vast plains and mountains, the state has different kinds of weather. The entire state experiences all four seasons, but some areas are more extreme than others. Heat waves and blizzards can strike, but pleasant weather is also common.

Path of the Continental Divide

Montana's average annual precipitation statewide is 19 inches (48 cm). In the mountains, on the western side of the Continental Divide, rain and snowfall are more plentiful. When warm breezes from the west rise over the mountains, moisture condenses and falls to the ground as rain or snow.

In Montana, rain and snow are more plentiful on the western side of the Continental Divide.

A woman walks down a path after a heavy Montana snowfall.

On the eastern side of the mountains and on the plains, the climate is more arid. The clouds moving overhead have already dropped most of their moisture over the western mountains.

Montana residents are famous for suffering through bitterly cold winters. The coldest temperature ever recorded in the 48 contiguous United States occurred at Rogers Pass on January 20, 1954. On that day, the thermometer sank to a bone-chilling -70°F (-57°C). Cold snaps, however, can be short lived. Warm breezes from the west, called Chinook winds, often ease the bitter winter temperatures.

CLIMATE AND WEATHER

PLANTS AND ANIMALS

The mountainous western side of Montana is mostly filled with forests. About one-fourth of the state is forestland. That is approximately 23 million acres (9.3 million ha). Common trees in this part of the state include larch, lodgepole pine, Douglas fir, spruce, western hemlock, and western red cedar. Ponderosa pine is the official state tree of Montana.

Trees cannot grow on the tallest mountain peaks. It is too cold and the land is too rocky. Snow may cover some areas all year long. The exact altitude of this "tree line" varies. In the northern Rocky Mountains, it is usually between 10,000-12,000 feet (3,048-3,658 m).

Mountain Goat

Above the tree line, there is alpine tundra vegetation similar to what is found in the far north. Grasses, lichens, and mosses cling to the ground. For the most part, rocks, snow, and glaciers cover this harsh landscape.

Mountain Lion

Grizzly Bear

Bighorn Sheep

Many large mammals make their home in the lower elevations of Montana's mountains. The state is famous for its grizzly bears, mountain goats, moose, and bighorn sheep. Other mammals include elk, black bears, gray wolves, mountain lions, bison, lynx, and bobcats.

PLANTS AND ANIMALS

The plains of eastern Montana have a semi-arid climate. Fewer trees grow in this part of the state, although there are pockets of forests. The most common trees are ponderosa and lodgepole pine. On prairie lands, vegetation includes prairie grasses, cactus, and sagebrush.

Some of the most common animals in the eastern part of the state include coyotes, rabbits, badgers, mule deer, and pronghorn.

Some animals are found all over the state. They include beavers, white-tailed deer, muskrats, and mink. Dozens of other small animal species can also be found.

Pronghorn

Snow geese and other waterfowl gather at Montana's Freezeout Lake.

Many kinds of birds can be spotted flying through Montana's skies. Bald eagles, ducks, and geese are often seen. The western meadowlark is the official state bird. In the spring, flocks of snow geese and tundra swans migrate through the state. Hundreds of thousands of these birds often gather at Freezeout Lake in north-central Montana.

There are 85 species of fish swimming in Montana's lakes, rivers, and streams. They include rainbow trout, northern pike, muskellunge, crappie, perch, sturgeon, and catfish. The blackspotted cutthroat trout is the official state fish.

There are many wildflowers native to Montana. They include primroses, lilies, sunflowers, orchids, bluebells, paintbrushes, and daisies. The official state flower of Montana is the bitterroot.

PLANTS AND ANIMALS

HISTORY

Before European explorers arrived, people had lived in today's Montana for at least 9,000 years or longer. These Paleo-Indians were the ancestors of today's Native Americans. They gathered plants and hunted large animals such as bison.

By the 1800s, several Native American tribes had established themselves all over the Montana area. In the mountainous west were the Kootenai, Salish, Kalispel, and Shoshone tribes. On the plains of eastern Montana were the Blackfeet, Gros Ventre, Assiniboine, Crow, Sioux, and Cheyenne people.

Blackfeet Native Americans in Glacier National Park in about 1920.

A painting by Edgar S. Paxson shows members of the Lewis and Clark Expedition at the Three Forks of the Missouri River. Individuals from left are John Coulter (hunter), York (Clark's slave), Meriwether Lewis, William Clark, Sacagawea (interpreter), and Charbonneau (interpreter and Sacagawea's husband).

The first European-Americans known to enter Montana were members of the Corps of Discovery, led by Meriwether Lewis and William Clark. The Lewis and Clark Expedition traveled through the area in 1805. They were exploring the vast Louisiana Purchase, which included Montana. They followed the Missouri River until crossing westward over the Rocky Mountains. They also passed through Montana on their journey home in 1806.

Within a few years after the Lewis and Clark Expedition, fur trappers began operating in Montana. Soon, forts were built to trade with Native Americans. The first permanent trading post was Fort Benton. It was built by the American Fur Company in 1846 along the Missouri River in north-central Montana.

Towns in Montana were created and shut down overnight when treasure hunters arrived and then left. Bannack is one of the best-preserved ghost towns in Montana.

Along with trappers and traders, missionaries began arriving in Montana in the early 1800s. Father Pierre-Jean De Smet was a Jesuit priest who founded St. Mary's Mission in 1841. Located near the Bitterroot River in west-central Montana, it is the oldest permanent settlement in the state. It was later renamed Stevensville.

In 1862, prospectors at Grasshopper Creek in southwestern Montana cried, "Eureka!" They had struck gold! Treasure hunters from all over the country flocked to Montana. Towns sprang up overnight. (When the gold later ran out, many towns were abandoned and became ghost towns.)

Following the gold rush, the United States created Montana Territory in 1864. Even more miners and settlers flowed into the area.

The Native Americans of Montana suffered as they began to lose their homes and hunting grounds. Some tribes signed peace treaties with the United States government and moved to reservations. On the reservations, however, many Native Americans were mistreated or neglected. They could no longer hunt on the open plains, as they had for generations. Some tribes decided to fight back.

From 1876-1877, Native Americans fought many battles and skirmishes against settlers and U.S. Army troops. The Lakota (Sioux) and Cheyenne tribes of Montana won their biggest victory at the Battle of the Little Bighorn in 1876 against troops led by Lieutenant Colonel George Custer. However, within a year, most of the Native Americans were disarmed and forced to live on reservations.

Lieutenant Colonel George Custer and his men were surrounded by thousands of Native American warriors during the Battle of the Little Bighorn in 1876.

After the wars with the Native Americans were over, cattle ranches appeared in greater numbers on Montana's open plains. As mining towns expanded, the residents wanted beef. Ranching became an important industry.

When railroads were built across the land in the 1880s, new farms and businesses were started, and the population expanded even more. Some Montana towns along the railroads, such as Billings and Miles City, became centers where cattle could be sent to markets in other states.

Montana cattle are loaded onto a train to be shipped to Chicago, Illinois.

The Anaconda Copper Mine in Butte, Montana, in 1903.

In the late 1880s, large deposits of silver and copper were mined near the town of Butte. More people flooded into Montana, seeking their fortunes.

In 1889, Montana became the 41st state to join the Union. The city of Helena became the capital. Joseph K. Toole was the state's first governor. Oil and gas were discovered in the early 1900s, boosting Montana's reputation as "The Treasure State."

Wheat farmers and cattle ranchers received good prices for their goods during World War I (1914-1918). However, hard times struck the state when the Great Depression began in 1929. Many people lost their jobs. A long drought further hurt wheat farmers. Big government projects in the 1930s helped put people back to work. During World War II (1939-1945), the economy began to recover.

Starting in the mid-1900s, mining became less important as deposits were depleted and environmental concerns were raised. Agriculture is still the state's biggest industry, but tourism greatly boosts the economy today. Visitors have discovered Montana's natural beauty.

DID YOU KNOW?

• On June 25-26, 1876, soldiers of the United States Army's 7th Cavalry battled warriors of the Lakota (Sioux), Northern Cheyenne, and Arapaho tribes near a small river in south-central Montana. It is known today as the Battle of the Little Bighorn. The Native Americans called it the Battle of the Greasy Grass, which was their name for the Little Bighorn River. The battle pitted the Army's Lieutenant Colonel George Armstrong Custer against Lakota Chief Sitting Bull, Crazy Horse, and thousands of their followers. Custer was brash. He rushed his troops into battle instead of waiting for reinforcements. He paid for his mistake with his life and the lives of more than one-third of the soldiers under his command, about 270 men in total. Between 60-100 Native Americans were also killed. The Native Americans had won their greatest victory in the struggle to keep their way of life. However, their triumph did not last long. Within a year after the battle, most of the Lakota and Cheyenne were hunted down, disarmed, and confined to reservations. The battle site today is preserved as Little Bighorn Battlefield National Monument.

• Montana holds the record for the greatest temperature swing in a 24-hour period. On January 14, 1972, the temperature started at a teeth-chattering -54°F (-48°C) in the town of Loma, Montana. But the very next day, the thermometer soared to 49°F (9°C)!

Pompeys Pillar

• Pompeys Pillar is a sandstone rock formation on the south side of the Yellowstone River near Billings, Montana. It is 150 feet (46 m) high. Captain William Clark, part of the Lewis and Clark Expedition, carved his name on the side of the pillar on July 25, 1806. The landmark is named after Jean Baptiste Charbonneau, the son of Native American expedition member Sacagawea. Clark nicknamed the boy "Little Pomp." The captain climbed up the side of the landmark and etched his own name and date into the soft sandstone. It is the only physical evidence of the expedition that still exists. The site is preserved today as Pompeys Pillar National Monument.

DID YOU KNOW?

PEOPLE

Jack Horner (1946-) is a world-famous paleontologist, a person who studies dinosaurs. He was born and raised in Shelby, Montana. He has made many important discoveries, including finding proof that dinosaurs had tight-knit families and protected their young. Horner was just eight years old when he discovered his first dinosaur bone. He suffers from a learning disability called dyslexia, and flunked out of college several times. However, he quickly became an expert on dinosaurs and wrote several books. The University of Montana awarded him an honorary college degree in 1986. Horner became the curator of paleontology at the Museum of the Rockies and a professor at Montana State University in Bozeman, Montana, before retiring from the university in 2016. He was the scientific advisor on the *Jurassic Park* movies, and the inspiration for the character Dr. Alan Grant.

Jeannette Rankin (1880-1973) was the first woman ever elected to the United States House of Representatives. She served two terms, from 1917-1919 and from 1941-1943. Born and raised on a ranch near Missoula, Montana, she graduated from the University of Montana in 1902. She became active in the suffragette movement, which fought to give women the right to vote. While representing Montana in Congress, Rankin fought tirelessly for women's rights and to end the practice of forcing children to work in factories. She was also a pacifist who hated war. She was the only legislator to vote against the United States declaring war against Japan in World War II. She never regretted her decision. She insisted that war "is a wrong method of trying to settle a dispute."

Brad Bird (1957-) is a filmmaker most famous for his animated work such as *The Incredibles* and *Ratatouille*. Born in Kalispell, Montana, Bird decided to become an animator at age 11 after a tour of Walt Disney Studios. He created his own animated short films as a teenager and attracted the attention of people at Disney. After working on *The Fox and the Hound*, he left Disney

and began working on several television series, including *The Simpsons*. He then directed 1999's *The Iron Giant*, which was widely praised. Bird then began working for Pixar Animation Studios. He directed 2004's *The Incredibles*, which won an Academy Award for Best Animated Feature. He followed that success with *Ratatouille* in 2007, and the live-action film *Mission: Impossible–Ghost Protocol* in 2011.

Charles Marion Russell (1864-1926) was one of the most famous painters of the American West. He was born in Missouri, but as a boy became fascinated with cowboys and mountain men. At age 16, he moved to Montana, where he found work on cattle ranches. He loved the state so much that he made it his lifelong home. He specialized in painting scenes of the Old West, including cowboys, Native Americans, and Western landscapes. His painting *Lewis and Clark Meeting the Indians at Ross' Hole* is displayed at the Montana state capitol in Helena. Russell was also a talented bronze sculpture artist. Today, the C.M. Russell Museum displays much of his artwork. It is located in Great Falls, Montana, where Russell lived and worked.

CITIES

Billings is the largest city in Montana. Its population is 108,869. It is in the south-central part of the state, on the shores of the Yellowstone River. The city began in 1877 as a steamboat stop along the river. When railroads came through in the early 1880s, the town grew quickly as a transportation hub. Today, Billings has a diverse economy that depends on many kinds of businesses. Agriculture, mining, construction, and transportation are important, but so are printing, business services, finance, and education. Montana State University Billings is just one of several colleges in the city. At Zoo Montana, visitors can see dozens of species of animals, including grizzly bears, bald eagles, and bighorn sheep.

Helena is the capital of Montana. Its population is 29,943. It is located in the west-central part of the state, near the Big Belt Mountains. The Missouri River flows just east of the city. Helena began as a mining camp in 1864 after gold was discovered in Last Chance Gulch. Even though the city began as a mining town, trade, transportation, and government jobs are also important today. There are dozens of historical buildings in the city, including the Cathedral of Saint Helena, which finished construction in 1924. Helena residents love outdoor sports. Activities include hiking, fishing, and skiing in nearby wilderness areas.

Great Falls is Montana's third-biggest city. It is in the west-central part of Montana. Its population is 59,152. The Lewis and Clark Expedition first entered the area in 1805 as they traveled up the Missouri River. They were forced to perform a month-long portage around a series of tall waterfalls, for which the city is named. Today, the falls have been tamed and turned into hydroelectric power. Great Falls is an important industrial center. The Lewis & Clark National Historic Trail Interpretive Center is a 25,000-square-foot (2,323-sq-m) museum on a bluff overlooking the Missouri River. The Montana State Fair is held each year at the city's Montana ExpoPark.

Display of the Lewis and Clark Expedition's portage.

Bozeman is in southwestern Montana, less than 100 miles (161 km) north of the entrance to Yellowstone National Park. The city's population is 41,660. It is named after John Bozeman, the pioneer who blazed the Bozeman Trail. There are many historical buildings downtown. Bozeman is the home of Montana State University, which enrolls more than 15,000 students. At the Museum of the Rockies, visitors can marvel at the biggest *Tyrannosaurus rex* skull ever found.

Missoula is Montana's second-largest city. It is located in west-central Montana near the Idaho border. Its population is 69,821. The city got its start as a trading post and U.S. Army fort in the 1860s and 1870s. Today, the University of Montana is the city's largest employer. Health care, construction, transportation, and forestry are other major industries. There are many festivals, museums, and historical sites in Missoula. The U.S. Forest Service's Missoula Smokejumper Base is also located in the city.

TRANSPORTATION

There are 74,933 miles (120,593 km) of public roadways in Montana. Interstate I-15 runs from the Canadian border in the north to Idaho in the south. Interstate I-90 travels generally east and west, stretching from the Idaho border to just east of Billings, where it turns south and exits at the Wyoming border. Interstate I-94 travels from Billings eastward to the North Dakota border.

One of the most scenic roads in the nation is U.S. Route 212, better known as the Beartooth Highway. This 68-mile (109 km) mountain road zigzags its way through southern Montana and northern Wyoming, with plenty of heart-leaping vistas along the way, until ending near the northeast entrance of Yellowstone National Park.

The Beartooth Highway has been called "the most beautiful drive in America."

Amtrak provides passenger service through northern Montana.

Railroads have been an important way to move people and goods since Montana's pioneer days. Today, there are eight freight railroad companies hauling cargo on 3,200 miles (5,150 km) of track. The most common goods carried by railroad include coal, refined oil products, farm products, chemicals, and lumber. Amtrak provides passenger service on the Empire Builder line, which runs through the northern part of the state.

Montana's busiest airports are Bozeman Yellowstone International Airport and Billings Logan International Airport.

TRANSPORTATION

NATURAL
RESOURCES

Montana has 27,500 farms and ranches operating on about 60 million acres (24 million ha) of land. That is almost 64 percent of Montana's total land area. Beef cattle are the most valuable livestock product. Wheat is by far the most valuable crop. Other leading crops include hay, barley, peas, lentils, potatoes, corn, and beans.

Mining has long been important to "The Treasure State." In the western mountain region are valuable deposits of copper, gold, silver, molybdenum, platinum, talc, limestone, and other minerals.

A high-country cattle roundup at the Lonesome Spur Ranch in Montana.

Completed in 1940, the Fort Peck Dam harnesses the power of the Missouri River to provide electricity to the area.

Montana also has large deposits of coal, oil, and natural gas. Most oil is found in the northeastern part of the state. Most of the state's coal is dug from large surface mines in southeastern Montana's Powder River Basin.

In addition to burning coal, Montana gets much of its energy from hydroelectric plants such as the Fort Peck Dam on the Missouri River. With 23 total hydroelectric dams, Montana is the fifth-largest producer of hydropower in the country.

The forests of western Montana provide wood for lumber. Douglas fir, ponderosa pine, and lodgepole pine are most often used to make products such as plywood, paper, and other wood products.

NATURAL RESOURCES

INDUSTRY

Montana is often called "the most rural state." Many people work in agriculture, raising beef cattle or growing wheat. However, approximately one-third of Montana's citizens work in the service industry. Instead of making products, service industries sell services to businesses and consumers. Montana's biggest service industries include education, health care, and finance. Many people are employed by the state and federal governments. The majority of the state's service industries are located in larger cities such as Billings, Butte, Great Falls, and Missoula.

Manufacturing employs about four percent of Montana workers. The state is home to more than 3,200 manufacturing businesses. They make items such as fabricated metal products, textiles, food products, machinery, petroleum and coal products, wood products, printing materials, furniture, and chemicals.

Huge fields of wheat are harvested at a farm near Havre, Montana.

Little Bighorn Battlefield National Monument is a popular historic site in Montana. Headstones, including Custer's, mark where U.S. Army soldiers and Native Americans died in battle.

Tourism has become a big business in Montana in recent years. Vacationers are attracted to the state's scenic beauty and the many outdoor activities available, including skiing, biking, fishing, and hunting. Millions of people each year visit Glacier and Yellowstone National Parks. There are also many popular historic sites in the state, including Little Bighorn Battlefield National Monument. The tourism industry supports more than 52,000 jobs in Montana and adds more than $3.6 billion to the state's economy.

SPORTS

Montana has too few people to support major league sports teams. However, several cities have minor league teams. Baseball is especially popular. The Billings Mustangs, Great Falls Voyagers, Helena Brewers, and Missoula Osprey all play in Minor League Baseball's Pioneer League.

High school and college sports are big in Montana. The University of Montana Grizzlies (often simply called "The Griz") and the Montana State University Bobcats are both part of the NCAA Division I Big Sky Conference. Each university has teams that play football, basketball, baseball, soccer, and other sports.

Cowboys, cowgirls, and Western heritage are an important part of life in Montana. Because of this, rodeos are very popular in the state. Events include bronc riding, steer wrestling, barrel racing, and bull riding. Dozens of rodeos are held each year across Montana.

A rodeo cowboy takes a fall at the annual Miles City Bucking Horse Sale.

A skier takes on Lone Peak at
Big Sky Resort near Bozeman, Montana.

Montana is famous for its scenic beauty and outdoor recreation opportunities. Top winter skiing and snowboarding destinations include Big Sky Resort and Bridger Bowl near Bozeman, and Whitefish Mountain Resort near Glacier National Park. Many other ski resorts are scattered throughout Montana's mountains. Other popular winter sports include snowmobiling and sled dog racing.

Montana has so many parks and wildlife refuges that there is something for everyone who loves outdoor sports. Hiking, camping, and backpacking are very popular in the summer months in Montana's vast wilderness areas. Fishing, hunting, and wildlife watching are also favorite activities.

SPORTS

ENTERTAINMENT

The Crow Fair is a yearly Native American festival held near Billings. Sponsored by the Crow Nation, it celebrates the culture of Great Plains Native Americans. Tens of thousands of people visit each year. Many other Native American festivals and dance celebrations, known as pow-wows, are held throughout Montana.

The Crow Fair is a yearly Native American festival held near Billings, Montana.

Bozeman's Museum of the Rockies features many dinosaur skeletons, as well as Native American and Montana history exhibits.

Bozeman's Sweet Pea Festival is a three-day gathering that celebrates the arts. First held in 1906 to honor the area's pea crop, the festival today includes Shakespeare plays, a parade, concerts, dance troupes, a flower show, and arts and crafts vendors.

The Museum of the Rockies in Bozeman, in addition to its Native American and Montana history exhibits, has the largest *Tyrannosaurus rex* collection in the world, plus many other dinosaurs. The museum also features a planetarium.

Helena's Montana Shakespeare Company features top actors from around the country performing full-length productions of William Shakespeare's plays in the capital city. Also in Helena is a museum and art gallery run by the Montana Historical Society.

TIMELINE

7000 BC—The first Paleo-Indians arrive in today's Montana area.

Pre-1800—Several Native American tribes are established in the Montana area, including the Kootenai, Salish, Kalispel, Shoshone, Blackfeet, Gros Ventre, Assiniboine, Crow, Sioux, and Cheyenne people.

1803—The United States buys much of present-day Montana from France in the Louisiana Purchase.

1805-1806—The Lewis and Clark Expedition explores the Montana area.

1841—St. Mary's Mission is founded. It is the first permanent settlement in Montana.

1846—Fort Benton is founded as a trading and military post.

1862—Gold is discovered at Grasshopper Creek in southwestern Montana. Treasure hunters begin pouring into the area.

1864—The federal government organizes Montana Territory.

1876—Lakota (Sioux) and Cheyenne Native Americans defeat Lieutenant Colonel George Custer and the United States Army's 7th Cavalry at the Battle of the Little Bighorn.

1880s—Railroads are built across the state, expanding trade and spurring many new businesses.

1880s—Large deposits of silver and copper are discovered near Butte. This leads to more prospectors and settlers moving into Montana.

1889—Montana becomes the 41st state in the Union.

1890—The first dam and hydroelectric facility is built on the Missouri River's Black Eagle Falls.

1940—The Fort Peck Dam is completed.

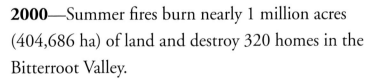

2000—Summer fires burn nearly 1 million acres (404,686 ha) of land and destroy 320 homes in the Bitterroot Valley.

2015—The Missoula Osprey win Minor League Baseball's Pioneer League championship.

GLOSSARY

Battle of the Little Bighorn

A battle in 1876 between the United States Army's 7th Cavalry, led by Lieutenant Colonel George Custer, and the Lakota (Sioux) and Cheyenne tribes of the Great Plains, fought near the Little Bighorn River in south-central Montana.

Contiguous

Connected or touching. For example, 48 of the 50 United States are contiguous. Alaska and Hawaii do not share borders with any of the other states.

Continental Divide

A ridge of the Rocky Mountains in North America. Water flowing west of the divide goes to the Pacific Ocean. Water flowing east eventually goes to the Atlantic Ocean.

Glaciers

Huge, slow-moving sheets of ice that grow and shrink as the climate changes. During the Ice Age, some glaciers covered entire regions and measured more than one mile (1.6 km) thick.

Great Depression

A time in American history, beginning in 1929 and lasting for several years, when many businesses failed and millions of people lost their jobs.

HYDROELECTRIC
A way of generating electricity that uses water to spin turbines instead of burning oil or coal.

LEWIS AND CLARK EXPEDITION
Explorers Meriwether Lewis and William Clark led an expedition from 1804-1806. Called the Corps of Discovery, the expedition explored the unknown territory west of the Mississippi River.

LOUISIANA PURCHASE
A purchase by the United States from France in 1803 of a huge section of land west of the Mississippi River. The United States nearly doubled in size after the purchase. The young country paid $15 million for approximately 828,000 square miles (2.1 million sq km) of land.

SMOKEJUMPERS
Firefighters who are trained to parachute out of airplanes in order to control and combat fires in remote, roadless wilderness areas.

WORLD WAR I
A war that was fought mainly in Europe from 1914 to 1918, involving countries around the world. The United States entered the war in April 1917.

WORLD WAR II
A conflict that was fought from 1939 to 1945, involving countries around the world. The United States entered the war after Japan bombed the American naval base at Pearl Harbor, in Oahu, Hawaii, on December 7, 1941.

INDEX